beetle bailey

by mort walker

A TOM DOHERTY ASSOCIATES BOOK

THE GREAT COOKIE CHASE!

FEELINGS

END

GUSTS

DOES THE FLOOR LOOK GOOD ENOUGH TO PASS INSPECTION WITHOUT HOSING IT DOWN WITH WATER?
SURE!

The
END

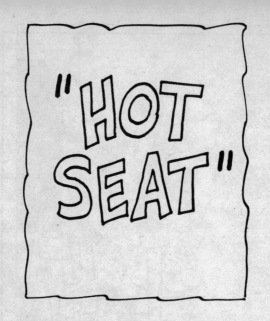

HMM--THE GENERAL IS OUT. I WONDER WHAT IT FEELS LIKE TO SIT BEHIND HIS DESK.

I'VE BEEN GONE AN HOUR AND MY CHAIR IS STILL WARM.

END

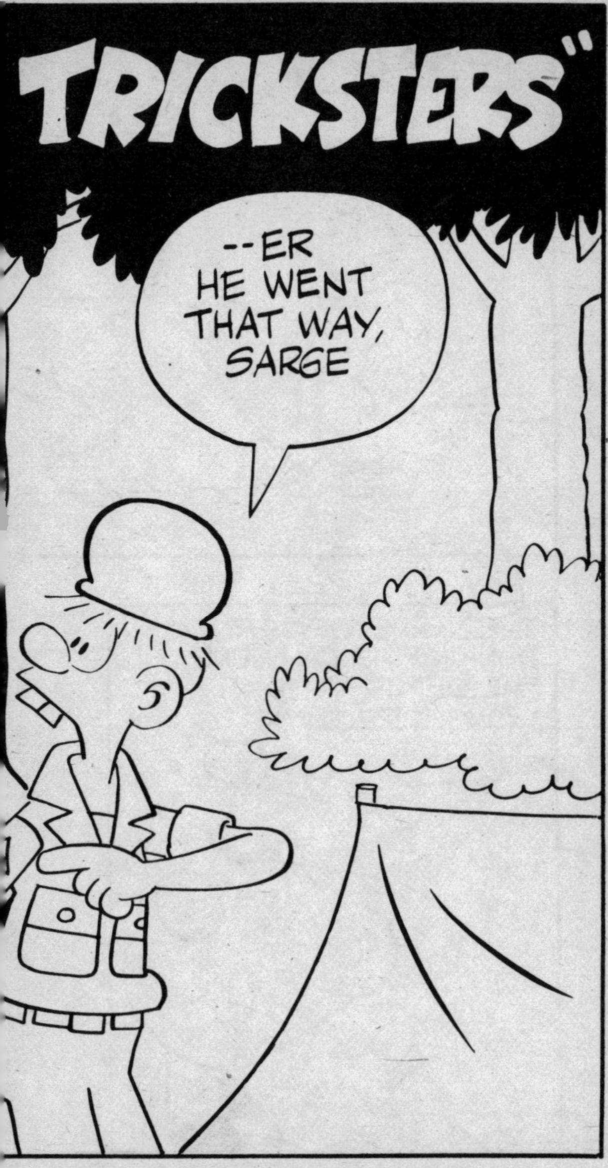
TRICKSTERS"
--ER HE WENT THAT WAY, SARGE

POW!